Book Map

Part I: The Shadow Over Seattle
- 1. The First Victim 1
- 2. The Body Count Rises 2
- 3. The Early Investigations 4
- 4. The Fear Takes Hold 5

Part II: The Hunt Begins 8
- 5. The Green River Task Force 8
- 6. The Evidence Trail 9
- 7. The Suspects Emerge 11
- 8. The Phantom Killer 14

Part III: The Capture 17
- 9. The Long Road to Gary Ridgway 17
- 10. The Breakthrough 18
- 11. The Confession 20
- 12. The Trial and Sentencing 22
- The Trial: A Mountain of Evidence 22
- The Aftermath: A Life of Imprisonment 24

Part IV: The Aftermath 25
- 13. The Impact of the Case 25
- 14. The Legacy of the Green River Killer 27
- 15. A Look at the Future 30

Part I: The Shadow Over Seattle

1. The First Victim

Introduce the discovery of the first victim, the chilling atmosphere in Seattle, and the initial confusion surrounding the case.

The summer of 1982 in Seattle was an idyllic blend of vibrant greenery and the intoxicating scent of blooming rhododendrons. The city, nestled between the emerald embrace of the Cascade Mountains and the shimmering waters of Puget Sound, was a picture of tranquility. However, beneath this veneer of serenity, a sinister shadow was beginning to emerge, casting an ominous chill over the Emerald City. It began with the discovery of a young woman's body, discarded in a desolate corner of the city, by the unforgiving banks of the Green River.

On July 8, 1982, a fisherman, casting his line in the murky waters of the Green River, stumbled upon a sight that would forever etch itself into the annals of Seattle's history. The body of Wendy Lee Coffield, a young, vibrant woman of 16, lay sprawled on the riverbank. Her lifeless eyes stared blankly at the indifferent sky, her once-bright smile now frozen in an eternal grimace. The discovery sent a shiver of dread through the city, igniting the spark of fear that would soon engulf Seattle.

In those early days, the police were bewildered. The crime scene offered few clues, leaving investigators grappling with an unsettling enigma. Coffield had been found in a secluded area, miles away from her home. Her body bore no obvious signs of struggle, and her purse and other belongings were missing. The lack of a clear motive or any readily identifiable suspect sent the police on a frantic chase down a labyrinth of unanswered questions.

Initially, the police dismissed the death as an isolated incident, a tragic accident perhaps, or the act of a desperate, lone wolf. The prevailing sentiment was that Seattle, with its reputation for being a safe and vibrant city, was immune to such horrors. But this was just the beginning. The discovery of Coffield's body would be the first of many, the opening act in a terrifying saga that would paint Seattle in the grim colors of fear and uncertainty.

2. The Body Count Rises

Detail the escalating fear and panic as more victims are found, establishing the pattern of the Green River Killer's modus operandi.

The discovery of Wendy Lee Coffield's body on July 8, 1982, sent shockwaves through Seattle. The initial confusion, the lingering scent of fear, and the sense of vulnerability that gripped the city were exacerbated by the discovery of another victim, Opal Mills, just a few weeks later. This time, the body was found in the Green River itself, a chilling echo of the river's name and the name that would forever be associated with the killer. With each subsequent discovery, the city's collective anxiety ratcheted up, transforming into a palpable fear that gripped the community. The "Green River Killer" had become a horrifying reality, a shadowy specter lurking in the shadows.

A chilling pattern began to emerge. The victims, all young women, were often found in remote locations, their bodies discarded like unwanted trash. The killer's preferred method was strangulation, leaving behind a chilling uniformity in the manner of death. Each new discovery brought a fresh wave of panic, as the chilling truth of the killer's modus operandi became increasingly clear. Fear became an insidious presence, altering the fabric of daily life. Women moved with an acute awareness of their surroundings, their steps echoing with the unspoken fear of becoming the next victim. The city, once known for its vibrant energy and youthful spirit, was now shrouded in a suffocating blanket of fear, a dark shadow cast by the unknown predator.

The **Green River Killer** wasn't just taking lives, he was stealing the city's peace of mind, its sense of safety. Each discovery fueled the media frenzy, transforming the killer into a mythical figure, a specter of terror that haunted the city's dreams. His anonymity and the lack of leads only intensified the fear, turning the victims into symbols of the unknown, their identities blurred into a collective sense of vulnerability. The city was in a state of siege, with the killer's presence felt in every corner, every street, and every shadow.

The pattern of the killings was both unsettling and terrifyingly consistent. The **Green River Killer** preyed on vulnerable women, often those who were marginalized or struggling with addiction. This pattern, while highlighting the killer's specific targets, also underscored the broader anxieties about safety and security in a rapidly changing society. It was a time when societal issues like homelessness, drug addiction, and sex work were seen as inextricably linked to the increasing crime rates, adding a layer of complexity to the narrative of fear.

3. The Early Investigations

Explore the challenges faced by the police in the early days of the investigation, the initial leads, and the mounting pressure to find the killer.

The initial investigation into the Green River murders was a daunting task for Seattle police. The victims, all young women, were found in various locations along the Green River, their bodies often discarded in remote areas. This presented an immediate challenge: the sheer scale of the crime scene. Unlike a murder committed within the confines of a home or apartment, the vastness of the river's banks made it incredibly difficult to search effectively. It became a race against time to secure evidence before it was lost to the elements or further compromised.

Further compounding the difficulty was the lack of a clear profile for the killer. In the early stages, the victims appeared to be unconnected, each with their own individual backgrounds and circumstances. This lack of a common thread made it challenging to identify any potential suspects, particularly in a city like Seattle, with its transient population and diverse neighborhoods. Each new discovery brought further complexity, with the investigation branching out to encompass various potential motives and avenues of inquiry.

Early leads were often fleeting and misleading. The initial focus was on known sex offenders and individuals with a history of violence against women, but the vastness of the potential suspect pool and the lack of a specific pattern made it difficult to narrow down the search. There were also numerous false leads and misdirection, which consumed valuable time and resources. The police faced immense public pressure to find the killer, with the media frenzy escalating with every new victim. This pressure created an environment of intense scrutiny, both on the police and on the investigation itself, potentially hindering their ability to pursue leads objectively.

The mounting pressure to find the killer was amplified by the growing fear in the community. The Green River murders had cast a dark shadow over Seattle, leaving women in particular feeling vulnerable and afraid. This fear was further exacerbated by the media's portrayal of the case, which often sensationalized the crimes and painted a terrifying picture of the killer's brutality. The constant news coverage fueled anxiety and created a climate of mistrust and suspicion. The police, under intense pressure, found themselves struggling to manage both the investigative demands and the public's need for reassurance and answers.

Despite the challenges, the detectives on the Green River Task Force persevered, meticulously piecing together the puzzle. They tirelessly followed leads, analyzed evidence, and interviewed countless individuals. Their determination and unwavering commitment, coupled with advancements in forensic science, would eventually lead to the capture of the Green River Killer, bringing an end to the terror that had gripped the city for nearly two decades.

4. The Fear Takes Hold

Document the impact of the killings on the Seattle community, the anxieties of women, and the changing landscape of fear.

The Green River murders cast a long, chilling shadow over Seattle, transforming the city's fabric and etching a permanent mark on the collective psyche of its residents. The once-vibrant, youthful metropolis became consumed by a pervasive sense of fear, a fear that seeped into every corner of life, chilling the air and transforming everyday experiences. For women, the fear was particularly acute, as they were the primary targets of the Green River Killer. The city, once a haven for young women seeking opportunity and adventure, now felt hostile and treacherous.

The murders began almost imperceptibly, the first few victims discovered in remote locations, their deaths initially dismissed as isolated incidents. However, as the body count rose, a terrifying pattern emerged, shattering the illusion of safety and unleashing a wave of panic throughout Seattle. The victims, predominantly young women, were often found near rivers and streams, their deaths marked by a brutal and chilling uniformity. The killer's modus operandi, his callous disregard for human life, sent shockwaves through the community.

The media, fueled by the public's thirst for information and their fear of the unknown, played a pivotal role in amplifying the terror. Headlines screamed of the "Green River Killer," painting a graphic picture of the horrors unfolding in their midst. The constant barrage of news and speculation fueled a sense of paranoia, turning everyday encounters into potential threats. Women became increasingly wary of their surroundings, constantly looking over their shoulders, their every step imbued with a sense of impending danger.

The fear extended far beyond the confines of the city, impacting the lives of women across the nation. The Green River Killer became a chilling symbol of the vulnerability of women, a terrifying reminder that danger could lurk anywhere, in the shadows of urban streets or the seemingly safe embrace of nature. Women, once accustomed to a sense of freedom and independence, found themselves bound by a newfound sense of caution, their lives circumscribed by fear.

The impact of the killings was not confined to the emotional realm. The Seattle community, once vibrant and thriving, became a place of suspicion and distrust. Neighbors, once friendly and familiar, became strangers, their every interaction tinged with unease. Families huddled closer, seeking solace in the familiar, while friendships strained under the weight of shared anxieties. The city, once a beacon of optimism and opportunity, now felt like a place of lurking shadows and unspoken fears.

As the investigation stretched on, the fear continued to fester, transforming the city's landscape into a place of constant vigilance. The Green River Killer's shadow loomed over Seattle, a chilling reminder of the fragility of life and the capacity for evil that lurked within the human heart. For those who lived through those harrowing years, the Green River murders remain a haunting chapter in their collective memory, a stark testament to the enduring power of fear and the profound impact of violence on a community.

Part II: The Hunt Begins

5. The Green River Task Force

Introduce the formation of the task force, the key individuals involved, and their initial strategies.

As the body count continued to climb, the Seattle Police Department was under immense pressure to find the Green River Killer. The initial investigations, while earnest, were hampered by a lack of resources and coordination. The sheer number of victims, coupled with the scattered locations of the bodies, overwhelmed the department. The frustration and anxiety of the public reached a boiling point, demanding action from law enforcement. In response to this mounting pressure and the growing realization that the Green River Killer was likely a serial offender, the Seattle Police Department took a decisive step: the formation of the Green River Task Force.

The Green River Task Force, assembled in 1982, represented a significant shift in strategy. Bringing together a select group of detectives, forensic experts, and criminal profilers, the task force was tasked with dedicating its sole focus to the investigation. The key individuals within the task force were instrumental in shaping the direction of the hunt.

Leading the charge was Detective Dave Reich, a seasoned investigator known for his relentless determination. His methodical approach and keen attention to detail would prove vital in unraveling the complex puzzle.

Joining Reich was Detective Robert Keppel, a former FBI agent with extensive experience in profiling serial killers.

The initial strategies of the Green River Task Force revolved around several key areas. The first and most critical was the comprehensive analysis of the crime scenes. Every piece of evidence, no matter how seemingly insignificant, was meticulously documented and analyzed by the forensic team. The task force's work included a deep examination of the victim profiles.

The Green River Task Force's initial strategies also included the development of a comprehensive victim database. This database, which would evolve over time, provided a central repository of information about each victim, including their personal lives, last known whereabouts, and any potential connections.

The task force also delved into the world of potential suspects. The initial suspects were primarily drawn from individuals with known histories of violence or those who had connections to the victims or the crime scenes.

The formation of the Green River Task Force marked a pivotal moment in the investigation. It represented a commitment to tackling the case with the necessary resources and expertise. While the path ahead would be fraught with challenges and setbacks, the task force's dedication and innovative approaches would eventually lead to significant breakthroughs in the hunt for the Green River Killer.

6. The Evidence Trail

Dive deep into the forensic evidence collected, the challenges of analyzing it, and the crucial breakthroughs in the investigation.

The Green River Killer case presented an unprecedented challenge for investigators, who had to navigate a complex web of evidence amidst the chilling reality of a growing body count. The killer's signature, a chilling pattern of dumping bodies in the Green River and nearby areas, offered a grim clue but lacked the definitive answers needed to crack the case. The early stages of the investigation were marked by a sense of urgency, as the fear in Seattle escalated with every new discovery. The detectives were tasked with collecting evidence, piecing together the fragmented clues, and navigating a landscape of uncertainty.

The evidence collected from the crime scenes was crucial, but it was far from straightforward. The bodies themselves, often found in advanced states of decomposition, presented their own challenges. The environmental factors of the riverbank, including wildlife and the changing water currents, often compromised crucial evidence. The and left behind were fragmented, making it difficult to draw concrete connections. was still in its early stages, leaving the investigators reliant on traditional methods like fingerprints and forensic anthropology to build their case.

As the investigation progressed, the Green River Task Force focused on several crucial areas of evidence. Autopsy reports provided valuable insights into the killer's modus operandi, revealing patterns of ligature strangulation and the use of various types of rope . The victims, mostly young women from vulnerable backgrounds, offered another crucial piece of the puzzle. The investigators compiled extensive victim profiles, seeking to identify commonalities

10

and potential links to a possible suspect. However, the lack of consistent evidence within the victims' backgrounds made it difficult to narrow down the search. Witness statements were also collected, but these were often incomplete or contradicted by other accounts, further complicating the investigation.

Despite the setbacks, the investigators pressed on. They developed an extensive database of potential suspects, cross-referencing various sources to identify possible connections. They meticulously analyzed the   , utilizing every resource available. The   of fibers and soil samples from the crime scenes offered crucial leads. The FBI was brought in to provide expertise, further bolstering the investigation. The public's help was also crucial, with numerous tips and leads pouring in from the Seattle community. The media coverage of the case, while it sometimes hampered the investigation, also generated valuable information and kept public interest high.

Despite the intensive efforts, the Green River Killer remained elusive for years. The lack of a definitive physical description of the killer, coupled with the lack of a consistent modus operandi, created a challenging investigative landscape. The evolving nature of the evidence added further complexity, requiring the investigators to constantly adapt their strategies and refine their analysis. However, the investigators persevered, driven by the victims and the determination to bring the killer to justice.

7. The Suspects Emerge

Explore the various suspects who emerged during the investigation, their connections to the case,

and the evidence that either connected or exonerated them.

The Green River Killer case, while eventually culminating in the arrest and conviction of Gary Ridgway, wasn't a straightforward investigation. For over a decade, detectives chased countless leads, scrutinized countless individuals, and meticulously pieced together fragments of evidence in a desperate bid to identify the man responsible for the horrifying string of murders. The investigation was plagued by a sense of urgency and a constant fear of the unseen, elusive killer. The sheer volume of victims, the varied locations of the bodies, and the seemingly random nature of the killings added layers of complexity to the case. The task force, burdened by the weight of the unsolved murders, knew they had to move quickly and decisively, but they also had to be meticulous in their approach. Every lead had to be thoroughly explored, and every suspect had to be investigated with utmost care.

The early investigations were marked by a desperate scramble for clues. The police were inundated with calls from concerned citizens, each with their own theories and suspicions. The fear and anxiety that gripped the Seattle community led to an atmosphere of heightened paranoia, making it difficult to distinguish between credible leads and unfounded rumors. However, as the years passed, the investigators narrowed their focus to specific suspects, often based on their proximity to the victims, potential motives, or criminal histories.

One of the early suspects was Ted Bundy, the infamous serial killer who was known to have operated in the Pacific Northwest. Bundy's modus operandi bore some similarities to the Green River Killer's, and his penchant for young women made him a prime suspect in the early stages of the investigation. However, investigators quickly ruled out Bundy as a suspect, noting that the locations of the Green River victims differed significantly from Bundy's typical hunting grounds. While Bundy's modus operandi involved luring victims with a disarming charm and a calculated approach, the Green River Killer, it seemed, targeted women who were often marginalized, vulnerable, and living on the fringes of society.

As the investigation progressed, the task force developed a profile of the Green River Killer, painting a picture of a man who was likely familiar with the Seattle area, had an intimate knowledge of the Green River corridor, and was possibly connected to the trucking industry. This profile, coupled with the growing evidence, led investigators to focus on several individuals who fit the description. One such suspect was Tommie Lee Andrews, a truck driver who had been convicted of rape and murder in 1982. Andrews, who had a history of violence against women, had been linked to several unsolved murders in the Pacific Northwest, including some that bore similarities to the Green River killings. The investigation into Andrews revealed a disturbing pattern of violence and a potential connection to the Green River case. However, the lack of conclusive evidence prevented investigators from formally charging him.

Another suspect who emerged early in the investigation was Robert Keppel, a former police officer who was known to have had a troubled past. Keppel had a history of violence against women, and his familiarity with the Seattle area made him a prime suspect. However, despite initial suspicions, investigators were unable to find any concrete evidence linking him to the Green River murders. Keppel's potential involvement in the case remained a subject of speculation for years, but he was eventually ruled out as a suspect due to a lack of compelling evidence.

The investigation was also hampered by the fact that the Green River Killer was meticulous in his efforts to avoid detection. He often disposed of the victims' bodies in remote locations, and he carefully cleaned up the crime scenes, leaving few traces of evidence. This meticulousness made it incredibly difficult for investigators to identify the killer. As the years went by, the pressure on the investigators mounted, and they found themselves constantly chasing leads that led to dead ends. One of the challenges faced by the investigators was the lack of a clear motive for the murders. The Green River Killer's victims were seemingly random, and there appeared to be no discernible pattern in their selection. This lack of a motive made it difficult to narrow down the suspect pool and to understand the killer's psychological makeup. The investigators also struggled with the fact that many of the victims were women who were marginalized and often overlooked by society. They were runaways, sex workers, and drug addicts – individuals who were often considered disposable by society. The killer's apparent disregard for these victims made it even more difficult to pinpoint him.

As the investigation dragged on, it became increasingly clear that the Green River Killer was a skilled and elusive predator. The task force, despite their tireless efforts, found themselves constantly outmaneuvered by the killer. The case seemed to slip through their fingers, and the frustration and disappointment began to weigh heavily on them. The Green River Killer, meanwhile, continued to operate with impunity, his identity shrouded in mystery.

8. The Phantom Killer

Delve into the psychological profile of the Green River Killer, analyzing the killer's motivations, personality traits, and likely background.

The chilling reality of the Green River murders demanded more than just a factual account of the killings; it required an exploration into the mind of the killer, a psychological dissection of the individual responsible for such horrific acts. The very nature of serial murder, characterized by a pattern of killings often separated by periods of normalcy, hinted at a complex and often deeply troubled psyche. The Green River Killer, whose reign of terror haunted Seattle for over a decade, presented a fascinating, and ultimately terrifying, puzzle for psychologists and investigators alike.

The **lack of a clear motive** in the Green River murders added a layer of mystery to the case. Unlike some serial killers driven by sexual gratification, financial gain, or religious beliefs, the Green River Killer's motivations seemed to defy easy categorization. This lack of a readily identifiable motive pointed to a more profound disturbance within the killer's psyche, a twisted internal landscape that fueled his actions. Early psychological profiles, constructed based on the available evidence and victim demographics, suggested a **deep-seated sense of anger and resentment towards women**, potentially stemming from personal experiences of betrayal or rejection. The killer's focus on women working as sex workers in Seattle's red-light districts hinted at a possible **link between his actions and a distorted sense of power and control**.

Beyond his motives, the Green River Killer's **personality traits** revealed a disturbing mix of **ordinary and extraordinary**. On the surface, Gary Ridgway, the man later identified as the Green River Killer, presented as a seemingly average individual. He held down a job at a car

15

painting shop, had a wife, and outwardly appeared to blend into society. However, beneath this veneer of normalcy lay a **dark undercurrent of narcissism, a need for control, and a deep-seated sense of anger and resentment**. He exhibited a **lack of empathy for his victims**, treating them as disposable objects, and displayed a **callous disregard for human life**. His **meticulousness in disposing of the bodies**, often going to great lengths to conceal them, further highlighted his need for control and his meticulous nature.

Delving into Ridgway's likely background, psychologists sought to understand the origins of his disturbing personality traits. His troubled childhood, marked by an abusive father and a distant mother, provided fertile ground for the development of antisocial tendencies. His experiences with violence and his limited emotional development could have contributed to his warped sense of morality and his capacity for cruelty. Moreover, his later experiences with voyeurism and prostitution further fueled his warped desires and distorted his view of women.

The psychological profile of the Green River Killer, while offering insights into the mind of a monster, ultimately remains a complex and unsettling picture. The very act of trying to comprehend the motivations and personality of a serial killer can be a deeply unsettling process, forcing us to confront the darkest corners of human nature. The Green River case serves as a chilling reminder that the veneer of normalcy can hide depths of depravity, and that even in seemingly ordinary individuals, the seeds of evil can take root and blossom into unimaginable acts.

Part III: The Capture

9. The Long Road to Gary Ridgway

Introduce Gary Ridgway, his seemingly ordinary life, and the events that led to his emergence as a prime suspect.

For years, the Green River Killer had haunted the streets of Seattle, leaving behind a trail of terror and unanswered questions. The investigation had consumed countless resources and had, at times, seemed destined to remain unsolved. But then, a seemingly ordinary man, living an unassuming life in a quiet suburban neighborhood, emerged as a prime suspect: Gary Ridgway.

Gary Ridgway, a truck painter, was a man who blended seamlessly into the background, appearing as unremarkable as the everyday objects he painted. His neighbors saw him as a quiet, unassuming man, a devoted husband, and a regular churchgoer. No one could have guessed that behind this seemingly harmless facade lurked a sinister secret. However, unbeknownst to the community, Ridgway was harboring a dark and violent side, one that would eventually be exposed through a complex and painstaking investigation.

Ridgway's emergence as a suspect began with a series of seemingly unrelated events. The first break came with the discovery of a crucial piece of evidence: a single hair. The hair, found on one of the victims, was painstakingly matched to a hair sample from Ridgway, obtained during a routine traffic stop. While this was a significant development, it wasn't enough to secure his arrest. The investigators needed more.

Adding to the intrigue, a key witness emerged: a former girlfriend of Ridgway's. She recalled a chilling story, one that involved a specific detail she had never disclosed to anyone before. She remembered that Ridgway had described a method for disposing of bodies, a method that mirrored the way the victims were found. This detail, coupled with the hair evidence, raised the stakes dramatically.

The investigation, now fueled by fresh evidence, intensified. The investigators meticulously analyzed Ridgway's life, examining his routines, his past, and his relationships. They discovered that Ridgway worked in a factory near the Green River, a location where several of the victims were found. Furthermore, investigators learned that Ridgway had a history of violent behavior, including past domestic abuse charges, adding weight to the suspicions surrounding him.

The pieces of the puzzle were slowly falling into place. Ridgway was no longer just an ordinary man, living an ordinary life. He was now a prime suspect, a man whose seemingly harmless existence concealed a horrifying truth. The weight of the investigation now rested heavily on the shoulders of law enforcement, as they prepared to confront the man they believed was the Green River Killer.

10. The Breakthrough

Detail the crucial pieces of evidence that finally connected Ridgway to the murders, including the DNA evidence and witness testimonies.

The long and arduous hunt for the Green River Killer finally yielded results in 2001, with the emergence of Gary Ridgway as the prime suspect. Years of meticulous investigation, tireless efforts by law enforcement, and the relentless pursuit of every lead had brought them to this point. However, it was a combination of crucial evidence, including DNA, witness testimonies, and meticulous detective work, that finally cracked the case wide open.

The breakthrough came with the advancement of DNA technology. In the early days of the investigation, DNA analysis was still in its infancy. The technology was not as sophisticated as it is today, and many of the early samples collected could not be definitively linked to any individual. However, as the technology progressed, detectives were able to revisit those samples and compare them to potential suspects, including Ridgway. In the late 1990s, a breakthrough occurred when a sample of sperm recovered from the body of one of the victims, Marcia Chapman, was tested and linked to Ridgway through a national DNA database. This match provided a crucial link between the suspect and a known victim.

This DNA evidence was further corroborated by several compelling witness testimonies. One particularly important piece of evidence came from a former girlfriend of Ridgway's, who came forward with a startling claim. She stated that Ridgway had confided in her, telling her that he was the Green River Killer and that he had disposed of the bodies of some of his victims near the Green River. This testimony was incredibly valuable, as it provided a strong link between Ridgway, his potential motive, and the location of the victims' bodies.

The investigation also unearthed crucial information from a former coworker of Ridgway's, who had noticed a peculiar pattern in his behavior. She testified that Ridgway had frequently spoken about prostitutes, and that he had expressed a disturbing fascination with their lives and lifestyles. This testimony provided further insight into Ridgway's possible motivations and the type of victims he targeted. It also pointed toward a possible connection to the Green River killings, as many of the victims were known to be sex workers.

With mounting evidence pointing toward Ridgway, the detectives began to close in on their suspect. Their meticulous work, the painstaking analysis of DNA evidence, and the crucial testimonies of witnesses all played a vital role in finally bringing the Green River Killer to justice. The capture of Gary Ridgway marked a significant moment in the history of criminal justice, not only for the families of the victims but also for the people of Washington state, who had lived in fear for so many years.

11. The Confession

Explore the process of Ridgway's arrest, his eventual confession, and the shocking details he revealed about his crimes.

The shadow of the Green River Killer had loomed over Seattle for over two decades. The apprehension of the man behind the murders felt like a distant dream, a glimmer of hope on the horizon that often seemed to fade with the setting sun. Yet, in November 2001, a breakthrough in the case sparked a flicker of excitement that quickly turned into a blazing fire of justice. The key to this sudden turn of events lay in a discarded cigarette butt found near the remains of one of the victims, a woman named Marcia Chapman. The DNA evidence extracted from the cigarette, a seemingly insignificant piece of discarded trash, would prove to be the missing link in the investigation. The DNA matched the profile of Gary Ridgway, a truck painter who had always remained a suspect in the eyes of law enforcement.

Ridgway's arrest on November 30, 2001, brought a wave of relief and a sense of closure to the community. The man who had haunted their nightmares for so long was finally in custody. Detectives Dave Reich and Tom Jensen, who had spent years chasing this elusive phantom, finally saw their relentless efforts bear fruit.

However, the arrest was just the beginning of the long road to justice. The real challenge lay in getting Ridgway to confess to the crimes and provide the details that would bring closure to the families of the victims. Detectives knew they needed more than just DNA evidence to secure a conviction; they needed a confession, a harrowing and unsettling account of the crimes from the killer himself. What followed was a complex psychological game of cat and mouse, a desperate search for truth in the darkest corners of the human psyche. The investigators employed a blend of psychological manipulation, carefully constructed scenarios, and meticulous legal maneuvering to encourage Ridgway to confess. They offered him a deal, the promise of a lesser sentence in exchange for his confession and cooperation.

The details that emerged from Ridgway's confession were chilling, a stark reflection of the evil that had lurked within him for so long. He revealed his predilection for picking up female sex workers, the way he manipulated and lured them to their deaths, the locations of their final resting places, and the horrifying methods he employed to silence his victims. In his own words, he painted a vivid picture of his crimes, a gruesome masterpiece of violence and depravity that sent shockwaves through the community. Ridgway confessed to killing at least 48 women between 1982 and 1998, making him one of the most prolific serial killers in American history. His confession was a chilling testament to the chilling truth that often lurks behind seemingly ordinary faces.

The story of Ridgway's arrest, confession, and sentencing is a complex and multi-layered account of the pursuit of justice. It is a story of the painstaking work of detectives, the dedication of prosecutors, the resilience of the community, and the enduring pain of the victims' families. It is a story that underscores the dark side of human nature, but also highlights the unwavering spirit of those who seek justice, even in the face of overwhelming darkness.

12. The Trial and Sentencing

Document the trial proceedings, the overwhelming evidence presented against Ridgway, and his ultimate sentencing to life imprisonment.

The Trial: A Mountain of Evidence

With Gary Ridgway in custody, the long-awaited trial began in 2003, captivating the attention of the nation. The courtroom became a battleground, where prosecutors relentlessly presented a mountain of evidence, meticulously connecting Ridgway to the horrific crimes. His life, once seemingly ordinary, was now laid bare, each detail meticulously examined under the harsh glare of the courtroom spotlight. The evidence presented was overwhelming, painting a chilling picture of the Green River Killer's reign of terror.

At the heart of the prosecution's case was the DNA evidence, collected from the victims and painstakingly analyzed. The DNA found on several victims matched that of Ridgway, proving a direct link to the crimes. The testimony of witnesses, including those who had encountered Ridgway in the past, also provided crucial support. They recalled his interactions, his demeanor, and his presence in the vicinity of where the victims were found, creating a chilling web of circumstantial evidence.

The prosecution also presented compelling evidence of Ridgway's confession, which he had given to police after his arrest. In the confession, Ridgway detailed the murders in graphic detail, describing how he lured his victims, how he strangled them, and how he disposed of their bodies. The confession was a powerful testament to the extent of his crimes and the level of depravity he displayed. While Ridgway later retracted his confession, the sheer weight of his own words, corroborated by the physical evidence, proved to be a devastating blow to his defense.

As the trial progressed, the defense team, while fighting a losing battle, attempted to cast doubt on the reliability of the evidence presented, arguing that it was circumstantial and that Ridgway's confession had been coerced. However, the jury was unconvinced, and after weeks of deliberation, they found Ridgway guilty on 48 counts of aggravated murder.

The sentencing hearing was a somber affair, marked by the emotional testimonies of the victims' families. They spoke of their pain, their loss, and the lasting impact the murders had on their lives. Ridgway, who had maintained his innocence throughout the trial, remained stoic, offering no apologies or expressions of remorse. The judge, in a powerful statement, recognized the gravity of Ridgway's crimes and sentenced him to 48 consecutive life sentences without the possibility of parole.

The Aftermath: A Life of Imprisonment

With the trial concluded, Ridgway's reign of terror finally came to an end. He was sent to a maximum-security prison, where he would spend the rest of his life, haunted by the ghosts of his victims and the weight of his crimes. The families of the victims, while finding some closure in the conviction, were left to grapple with the enduring pain of their loss.

The Green River Killer case left a lasting legacy on the Seattle community and the criminal justice system. It highlighted the importance of thorough investigation, forensic evidence, and the determination to bring serial killers to justice. The case also served as a stark reminder of the vulnerability of women, the lasting impact of violent crime, and the need for ongoing efforts to prevent such tragedies from occurring again.

Part IV: The Aftermath

13. The Impact of the Case

Explore the long-term effects of the Green River murders on the Seattle community, the families of the victims, and the criminal justice system.

The Green River murders cast a long, dark shadow over Seattle, leaving behind a legacy of fear, grief, and a profound sense of vulnerability. The city, once known for its vibrant energy and natural beauty, became synonymous with the chilling reality of a serial killer lurking in their midst. The impact of the crimes reverberated throughout the community, etching itself into the collective memory of Seattle and leaving an indelible mark on the families of the victims and the criminal justice system itself.

For the families of the victims, the Green River murders were a nightmare that never ended. They were forced to confront the unimaginable loss of their loved ones, their lives forever shattered by the cruel hand of a murderer. The pain of their grief was compounded by the agonizing uncertainty of the investigation, the constant fear of the killer remaining at large, and the public scrutiny they faced. Many families struggled with the media attention, feeling their loved ones' memories were being exploited for sensationalism. The prolonged nature of the investigation, spanning decades, kept the wounds fresh, delaying the closure they desperately craved.

The murders also left a deep sense of fear and distrust within the Seattle community. Women, in particular, felt vulnerable and apprehensive, altering their routines and taking precautions that had never seemed necessary before. The city's social fabric was frayed as people became more isolated and suspicious of strangers. The pervasive fear, fueled by the lack of information about the killer, permeated the community, creating a sense of unease that lingered for years. The "Green River Killer" became a chilling reminder of the fragility of life and the dark underbelly of society.

The Green River murders also exposed the limitations of the criminal justice system at the time. The initial investigations were hampered by a lack of resources, a fragmented approach, and a failure to recognize the pattern of the murders. This led to a frustrating delay in identifying the killer, allowing him to continue his rampage for years. The case also highlighted the need for improved communication and coordination among law enforcement agencies, particularly when dealing with complex serial crimes.

However, the Green River murders also sparked a significant evolution in the criminal justice system. The case led to the development of new investigative techniques, such as DNA profiling and psychological profiling, which proved invaluable in solving future crimes. The creation of dedicated task forces, specifically designed to tackle serial crimes, became standard practice, emphasizing the need for a more focused and collaborative approach. The Green River murders served as a wake-up call for law enforcement agencies, forcing them to adapt and improve their strategies in the face of evolving criminal threats.

The legacy of the Green River murders is complex and multifaceted. While the crimes left behind a trail of pain and fear, they also served as a catalyst for significant changes in the criminal justice system, leading to advancements in investigative techniques and a greater awareness of the challenges posed by serial crimes. The story of the Green River Killer is a chilling reminder of the darkness that can exist within society and the importance of vigilance, collaboration, and a commitment to seeking justice for all victims.

14. The Legacy of the Green River Killer

Analyze the enduring legacy of Gary Ridgway, the lessons learned from the case, and the ongoing efforts to understand and prevent serial killers.

The capture of Gary Ridgway, the Green River Killer, brought a sense of closure to a city haunted by fear. Yet, his story continues to cast a long shadow, leaving behind a complex legacy that compels us to grapple with the dark recesses of the human psyche and the ever-evolving dynamics of crime and justice.

One of the most enduring legacies of the Green River Killer case lies in the lessons learned about the nature of serial killers. Ridgway's seemingly ordinary facade, coupled with his chilling confession detailing the meticulous planning and calculated execution of his crimes, shattered the myth of the "monster" stereotype. The case revealed that serial killers can blend seamlessly into society, often exhibiting traits that make them appear unremarkable. This insight has profoundly shaped the understanding of criminal profiling, pushing investigators to adopt a more nuanced approach to understanding the motives and behaviors of these offenders.

Furthermore, the case highlighted the importance of forensic evidence in solving serial murder cases. The advancements in DNA technology played a crucial role in connecting Ridgway to the murders, a testament to the power of scientific advancements in criminal investigations. The Green River Task Force faced immense challenges in collecting and analyzing the vast amounts of evidence, but their persistence ultimately proved decisive. This success served as a crucial turning point in the field of forensic science, underscoring its increasing significance in identifying perpetrators and achieving justice.

However, the Green River Killer case also revealed the limitations of law enforcement in dealing with these complex crimes. The initial investigations were marked by missteps and failures to connect the dots, leading to the tragic loss of innocent lives. The case exposed systemic shortcomings, particularly in terms of communication, coordination, and the lack of a dedicated task force dedicated to serial killers. This realization has led to significant reforms in the approach to serial murder investigations, emphasizing the need for specialized units, improved interagency communication, and a more proactive strategy to prevent future tragedies.

The Green River Killer case also generated crucial insights into the psychological motivations behind serial murders. Ridgway's confession revealed a complex web of underlying factors, including his troubled childhood, his fascination with sexual violence, and his deep-seated desire for control. This complex interplay of factors challenged the simplistic explanations often attributed to serial killers, compelling experts to explore the multifaceted nature of these crimes and the psychological profiles of the individuals who commit them. This renewed focus on understanding the individual motivations of serial killers has been instrumental in developing more effective intervention strategies and rehabilitative programs.

Beyond its impact on criminal investigations, the Green River Killer case has also profoundly shaped the public's understanding of serial murder. The case's extensive media coverage, from newspapers and television news to documentaries and true crime books, has propelled the topic into the public consciousness. This heightened awareness has led to a greater understanding of the dangers posed by serial killers, as well as a growing demand for effective measures to prevent these crimes. The case serves as a stark reminder of the vulnerability of individuals and communities, prompting a national conversation about the need for enhanced safety measures and the importance of crime prevention programs.

However, the legacy of the Green River Killer is not without its controversies. The case also sparked debates about the death penalty, with some arguing that Ridgway's crimes warranted the ultimate punishment while others advocated for life imprisonment. These debates continue to be a source of division in society, highlighting the complex moral and ethical issues surrounding capital punishment. The case also raised concerns about the use of plea bargains in high-profile cases, leading to questions about whether justice was truly served. The Green River Killer case remains a reminder that justice is not always clear-cut and that the pursuit of justice can be fraught with ethical complexities.

Despite these challenges, the Green River Killer case stands as a testament to the enduring spirit of human resilience and the pursuit of justice. The unwavering commitment of the investigators, the courage of the victims' families, and the dedication of the community all played a vital role in bringing Ridgway to justice. The case serves as a reminder that even in the face of unimaginable darkness, hope and justice can prevail. It underscores the critical importance of collaboration, innovation, and unwavering determination in confronting the most challenging crimes of our time.

The Green River Killer case continues to shape the landscape of criminal justice and criminology, pushing experts and investigators to refine their understanding of these complex crimes. The legacy of Gary Ridgway is a sobering reminder of the darkness that lurks within society, but it is also a beacon of hope, demonstrating the power of collaboration, persistence, and the unwavering pursuit of justice. The case serves as a catalyst for ongoing efforts to understand and prevent serial murder, ensuring that the lessons learned are never forgotten and that the victims' stories continue to inspire hope and resilience.

15. A Look at the Future

Reflect on the future of true crime investigations, the evolving landscape of forensic science, and the ongoing quest to solve unsolved cases.

The chilling saga of the Green River Killer, a story that gripped Seattle and transfixed the nation, serves as a stark reminder of the enduring power of true crime investigations. As we reflect on the past, we must also look towards the future, envisioning how these investigations will evolve in the years to come. The Green River case itself showcases the critical role of forensic science in unraveling complex crimes, but it also underscores the need for continual innovation and adaptation. The landscape of forensic science is constantly changing, with advancements in DNA analysis, digital forensics, and other cutting-edge techniques promising unprecedented breakthroughs in solving cold cases.

The future of true crime investigations will be shaped by the integration of these technologies. Advanced DNA analysis, for instance, allows investigators to generate profiles from even the smallest traces of biological material, potentially linking suspects to crimes even decades later. The rise of digital forensics has revolutionized the way evidence is collected and analyzed. From recovering deleted files on computers to tracking online activity, digital forensics provides valuable insights into the minds and actions of criminals. The integration of artificial intelligence (AI) promises to further revolutionize the field, with AI-powered systems capable of analyzing massive datasets, identifying patterns, and generating leads that would have otherwise been missed.

However, alongside the technological advancements, it is essential to acknowledge the human element that remains crucial to solving true crimes. The relentless pursuit of justice, the painstaking dedication of investigators, and the unwavering commitment of victims' families are often the driving forces behind successful resolutions. The Green River case stands as a testament to the unwavering dedication of law enforcement professionals, who tirelessly followed every lead, analyzed every piece of evidence, and never gave up hope of bringing the killer to justice.

Looking ahead, the future of true crime investigations will also be marked by a renewed emphasis on community engagement. The public plays a vital role in solving crimes, providing vital information and collaborating with investigators. Engaging the public through proactive communication, community outreach programs, and innovative platforms for sharing information will be critical for fostering trust and garnering valuable assistance in solving cold cases.

The quest to solve unsolved cases is an ongoing endeavor, demanding the combined efforts of technology, human ingenuity, and community collaboration. The Green River Killer case serves as a powerful reminder of the human cost of crime and the importance of pursuing justice, no matter how long it takes. As we move forward, embracing innovation, strengthening partnerships, and prioritizing compassion, we can continue to unravel the mysteries of the past and ensure that no crime goes unpunished.

Printed in Great Britain
by Amazon